8/13

Teen

D0745450

KYLE BUSCH

by Matt Scheff

NASCAR
HEROES

Published by ABDO Publishing Company, PO Box 398166, Minneapolis, MN 55439. Copyright © 2013 by Abdo Consulting Group, Inc. International copyrights reserved in all countries. No part of this book may be reproduced in any form without written permission from the publisher. SportsZone™ is a trademark and logo of ABDO Publishing Company.

Printed in the United States of America,
North Mankato, Minnesota
112012
012013

Editor: Chrös McDougall
Series Designer: Becky Daum

Photo Credits: Autostock/Brian Czobat/AP Images, cover, title; Autostock/ Nigel Kinrade/AP Images, cover; Wade Payne/AP Images, 4-5; Ernie Masche/ AP Images, 6; Mark Humphrey/AP Images, 6-7, 22-23; Cal Sport/AP Images, 8-9, 24-25, 28-29; Chuck Burton/AP Images, 10-11, 30 (bottom, right); Jamie Belk/AP Images, 12-13; Tom Puskar/AP Images, 14-15; Dick Whipple/ AP Images, 16-17, 30 (top); Jae C. Hong/AP Images, 16; Jim Cole/AP Images, 18-19; Bill Friel/AP Images, 20-21; Rainier Ehrhardt/AP Images, 23, 30 (bottom, left); Autostock/Matthew T. Thacker/AP Images, 26-27, 31

Cataloging-in-Publication Data
Scheff, Matt.
 Kyle Busch / Matt Scheff.
   p. cm. -- (NASCAR heroes)
Includes bibliographical references and index.
ISBN 978-1-61783-660-2
1. Busch, Kyle--Juvenile literature. 2. Stock car drivers-- United States--Biography--Juvenile literature. I. Title.
796.72092--dc21
[B]

2012946249

CONTENTS

WEEKEND SWEEP

The fans at Bristol Motor Speedway stood. The 2010 National Association for Stock Car Auto Racing (NASCAR) Sprint Cup race entered its final laps. Some fans cheered. Others booed. But everyone was watching Kyle Busch's No. 18 Toyota.

Kyle Busch cruises around the track at Bristol Motor Speedway in Tennessee in 2010.

Busch celebrates his Sprint Cup win at Bristol Motor Speedway in 2010.

Entering 2012, Kyle Busch had more Sprint Cup wins (five) at Bristol Motor Speedway than at any other track.

Busch had already won the weekend's truck race and the Nationwide Series race. No driver had ever swept all three events in a weekend. Busch and David Reutimann battled for the lead. Busch finally got in front. He cruised across the finish line for the win. "I can't believe it!" he shouted. It was time to celebrate.

7

BORN TO RACE

Kyle Thomas Busch was born May 2, 1985, in Las Vegas, Nevada. Cars and racing were part of Kyle's life from the start. His dad, Tom Busch, competed in short-track races. Tom also liked to build and fix cars. Kyle and his older brother, Kurt, spent hours in the garage with their father.

Kurt Busch (1) and Kyle Busch (54) race against each other in a Nationwide Series race in 2012.

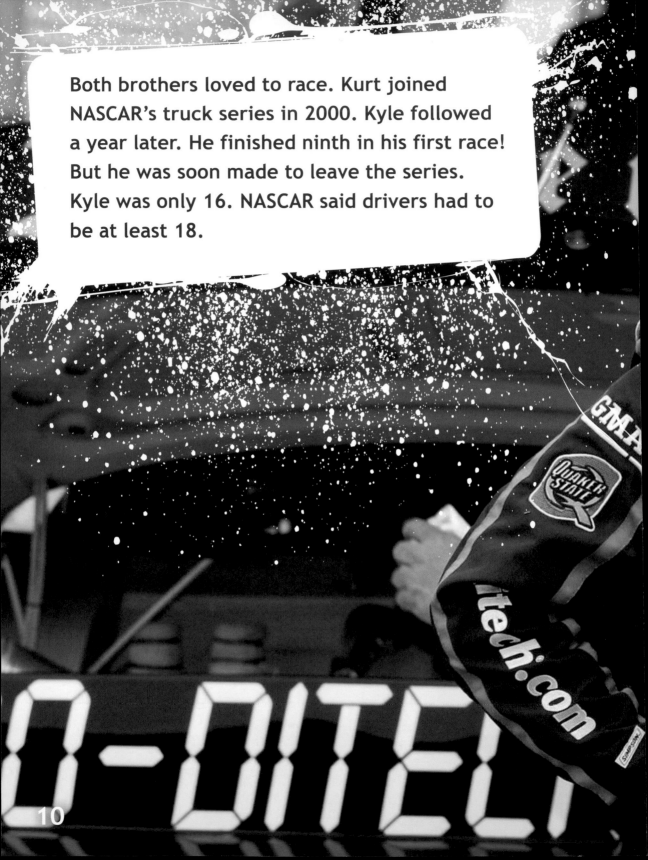

Both brothers loved to race. Kurt joined NASCAR's truck series in 2000. Kyle followed a year later. He finished ninth in his first race! But he was soon made to leave the series. Kyle was only 16. NASCAR said drivers had to be at least 18.

Kyle in 2003 at age 18

FAST FACT

As a teen, Kyle Busch had to pay for his own race cars. His dad believed Kyle would learn to take better care of them that way.

FINDING A RIDE

Busch drove in the American Speed Association (ASA) racing series. He finished eighth in ASA points in 2002. Many NASCAR teams were interested in signing Busch. He decided to sign with Hendrick Motorsports in 2003. Busch turned 18 in May. He started driving in NASCAR's second-level series that year. He finished second in his first race!

FAST FACT
Many expected
Kyle Busch to join
Kurt Busch on the
Roush Racing team.
Kyle said he signed
elsewhere to step out
of Kurt's shadow.

*Busch (22) escapes a
wreck during a 2002
race in North Carolina.*

13

MOVING ON UP

In 2004, Busch won his first second-level series race. He started driving in the Cup Series the next year. His first Cup win came September 4 at California Speedway.

FAST FACT

In 2004, Kyle Busch was named Rookie of the Year in NASCAR's second-level series. In 2005, he was named Rookie of the Year in the Cup Series.

Busch celebrates a second-level series win in 2004.

In 2006, Busch made the Chase for the Cup for the first time. He finished tenth. Busch made the Chase again in 2007. This time, he finished fifth.

Kyle, left, and Kurt Busch in 2007

*Busch approaches the finish
line at a 2007 second-level
series race in Kansas.*

RECORD SETTER

Busch joined the Joe Gibbs Racing team in 2008. He drove the No. 18 car. Busch had a great season. He won eight Sprint Cup races. He also won 10 Nationwide Series races and three truck races. His 21 wins that year were a NASCAR record.

Busch starts at the front of a 2008 race in New Hampshire.

Busch's car (18) shoots flames as he avoids a wreck during the 2012 Daytona 500.

NASCAR'S BAD BOY

Busch was having lots of success. But many fans disliked him. They thought he was cocky and hotheaded. Busch got into feuds with drivers such as Carl Edwards and Kevin Harvick. Many fans saw him as a villain.

Busch often encouraged the fans to boo. He said he was just glad that they were making noise. He said he would rather they boo him than ignore him.

FAST FACT

In a 2010 poll, fans voted Kyle Busch NASCAR's least popular driver.

Busch leads Mark Martin in the final lap at Bristol in 2009.

HIGHS AND LOWS

Busch dominated the Nationwide Series in 2009. He won nine races and the championship. But he struggled in Sprint Cup. He missed the Chase and finished thirteenth.

Busch won 13 Nationwide Series races in 2010. From May to July, he won six out of seven races. He also won three Cup races and made the Chase. But he struggled in the Chase and finished eighth.

FAST FACT

Kyle Busch formed Kyle Busch Motorsports in 2009. Both Kyle and Kurt Busch have driven Nationwide Series races for the team.

Busch celebrates a 2009 truck series win.

23

FINDING TROUBLE

Busch's 2011 season started great. He was leading the point standings. But he was also getting into trouble. He almost got into a fight with Kevin Harvick. Then Busch wrecked another driver on purpose at a truck race. NASCAR banned him from racing for the rest of the weekend, including the Sprint Cup race. The punishment ended his title hopes. His great start had turned to disaster.

Busch (18) and Kevin Harvick (29) battle for position during a 2011 race in Virginia.

WILD TALENT

Fans never know what to expect from Busch. He has been one of the sport's best drivers. But he is also known to blow up at any moment.

Through 2012, Busch had won more than 100 races in NASCAR's three major series. That put him on pace to become NASCAR's all-time wins leader someday.

Kyle Busch (18) and Kurt Busch (51) race side-by-side in a 2012 race.

27

Busch took NASCAR by storm as a teenager. He has been one of the world's best stock car drivers ever since. As of 2012, one of the few accomplishments Busch had yet to achieve was a Sprint Cup title. But with Busch behind the wheel, it appears to only be a matter of time.

Busch celebrates a preseason win at Daytona International Speedway in 2012.

1985
Kyle Thomas Busch is born on May 2 in Las Vegas, Nevada.

2001
Busch races in his first NASCAR truck race. He finishes ninth.

2003
Busch joins Hendrick Motorsports.

2004
Busch wins his first second-level series race at Richmond International Raceway on May 14.

2005
Busch starts racing in the Cup Series full-time and wins his first race on September 4 at California Speedway.

2008
Busch joins Joe Gibbs Racing. He wins a NASCAR record 21 races that year.

2009
Busch wins nine Nationwide Series races and the championship.

2011
NASCAR suspends Busch after he intentionally wrecks Ron Hornaday in a truck race.

GLOSSARY

Chase
The last 10 races of the NASCAR Cup series. Only the top 10 drivers and two wild cards qualify to race in the Chase.

Cup Series
NASCAR's top series for professional stock car drivers. It has been called the Sprint Cup Series since 2008.

rookie
A driver in his or her first full-time season in a new series.

second-level series
NASCAR's second-level series for professional stock car drivers. It has been called the Nationwide Series since 2008.

series
A racing season that consists of several races.

stock car
Race cars that resemble models of cars that people drive everyday.

truck series
NASCAR's third national racing series. It has been called the Camping World Truck Series since 2009.

villain
A bad guy.

INDEX